Music for Amelia

A Play

Derek Rhodes

A SAMUEL FRENCH ACTING EDITION

SAMUEL FRENCH

FOUNDED 1830

SAMUELFRENCH-LONDON.CO.UK
SAMUELFRENCH.COM

MUSIC FOR AMELIA

First presented by the Company of Ten at the Abbey Theatre, St Albans, on 3rd July 1998, with the following cast:

Max	David Griffiths
Hector	Stephen Aitken
Messenger	Derek Rhodes

Directed by Norma Jenkins

Subsequently presented in 2004 by the Company of Ten at the following Drama Festivals: Letchworth (where it won the Best New Play award); Cambridge; South-West Herts; and Welwyn, with the following cast:

Max	Roy Bookham
Hector	Tim Robinson
Messenger	Bec Linton

Directed by Ro Linton

CHARACTERS

Max, a long-standing MP, a well-known figure in public life; mid 60s
Hector, an interrogator; mid 30s to mid 40s
Messenger, male or female; between 30 and 60

The action of the play takes place in an office

Time: the late 1990s

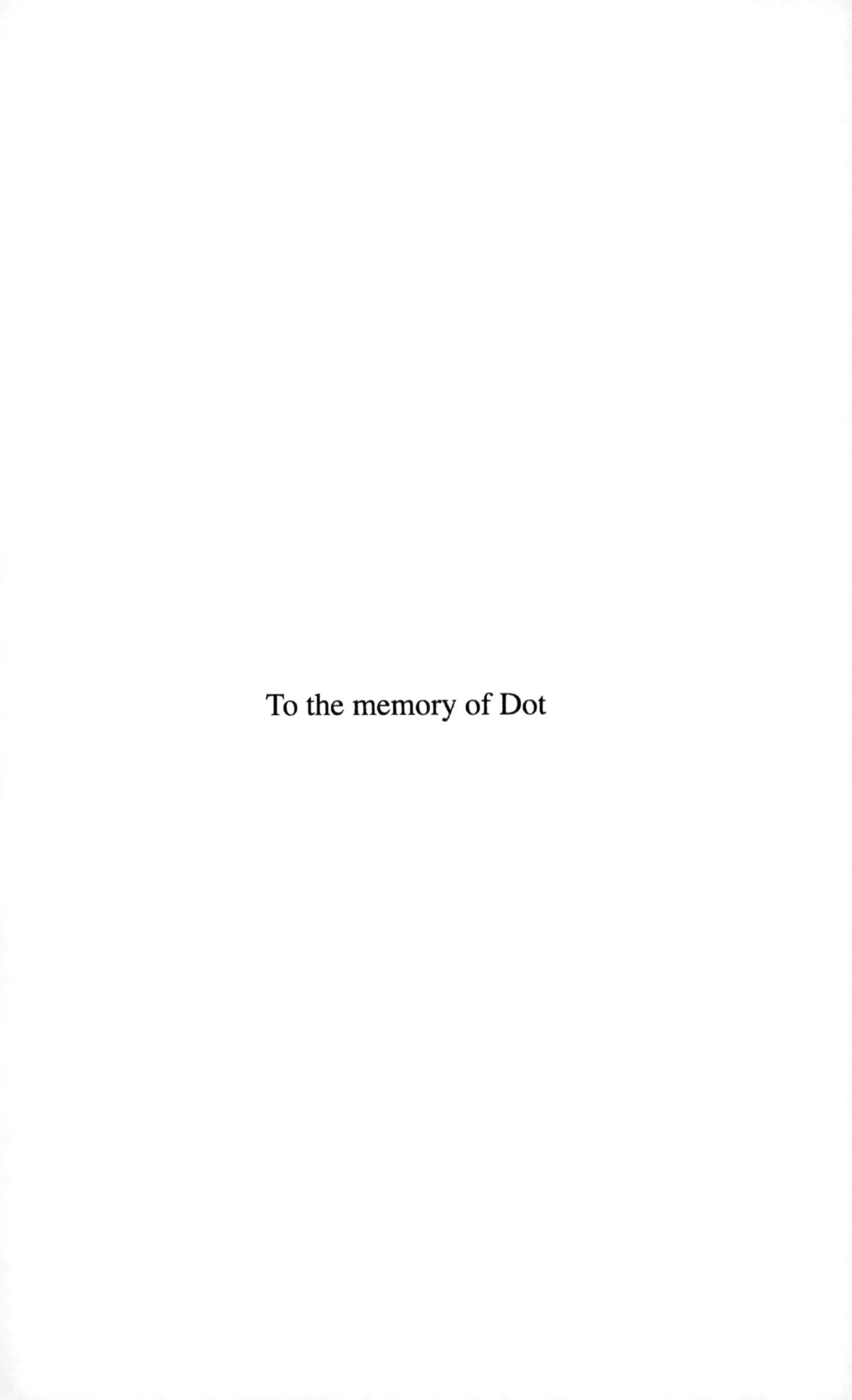

To the memory of Dot

MUSIC FOR AMELIA

An office. The late 1990s

The room is furnished with a desk and two chairs and there is a coatstand by the door with Max's overcoat hanging on it. On the desk are a lamp, a telephone, a tape machine and a water jug with glasses. Max's case stands on the floor. The room has no access to natural light; the only illumination comes from the lamp

The Prelude to Act I of "La Traviata" (Verdi) plays over the theatre speakers

The CURTAIN *rises. The desk lamp is on. Max is sitting on one side of the desk, reading the "Financial Times", but it is clear that he is not concentrating. He looks at his watch, then, with obvious annoyance, gets up, puts the newspaper down and paces about the room. He looks at his watch again and, with sudden determination, retrieves his paper, puts it in his case, goes to the coatstand, takes his coat from it and starts to put it on*

The door opens and Hector enters. He wears a suit with a handkerchief in the breast pocket and carries an official-looking file

The music fades

Hector So sorry to have kept you waiting, Sir Max. (*He holds out a hand*) I'm Hector. It's a great honour to meet you.
Max (*ignoring the proffered hand*) I was on the point of leaving. I do have ——
Hector Important business to attend to? Of course you do. Unforgivable, keeping you waiting.

Max And if that weren't bad enough, I'm forced to wait in this grubby little room. Is this how you usually treat people of my … Well, my … ?

Hector Standing?

Max Yes. No point in false modesty. I do have certain standing in the public affairs of this country.

Hector Indeed you do. A very considerable standing. You are a particularly important catch for the programme, if I may be allowed to say so.

Max Well, you certainly have a strange way of showing it. One minute more and your particularly important catch would have gone. Where would you have been then?

Hector Where indeed? (*He holds up the file*) Papers went missing.

Max (*puzzled*) Papers?

Hector Absolutely. Misplaced by some stupid clerk. Bloody place runs on paper. Lose the papers and everything stops.

Max But what papers?

Hector Background. Press cuttings, that sort of thing. She's very hot on background research.

Max Well, I hope she won't be long. I really will have to be going soon.

Hector She? You mean Amelia? But she's not coming.

Max Not coming? Who does she think she is? First she says she'll come to the flat, to talk about the show; I set aside yesterday evening …

Hector Yesterday? But I thought … (*He checks himself*)

Max I may say the arrangement put me to considerable inconvenience. And she couldn't even be bothered to tell me she wasn't coming.

Hector She didn't turn up?

Max You know bloody well she didn't. And don't think that sending a car for me this morning in any way mitigates the discourtesy. I can tell you, I nearly washed my hands of the whole business.

Hector It's just that ——

Max Bloody media people — all the same — think they run the world.

Hector I'm sure there was a good reason for her failure to keep the appointment. It's certainly most uncharacteristic of her not to have let you know. (*Pause*) I hope, at least, you were able to salvage something from the evening.

Max Bit late to make new arrangements.

Hector So how did you spend the time?

Max I ... (*Clearly having difficulty remembering*) I ... (*Giving vent to his frustration*) What the hell's it got to do with you? (*The lapse of memory continuing to nag him*) If you must know ... (*With sudden conviction*) If you must know, I listened to some music. Don't get much opportunity just to listen these days.

Hector Excellent! So it wasn't a complete waste. And music is what we're here to talk about.

Max But I had been expecting to be discussing the programme with Ms Cruikshank, not some junior ——

Hector I should have been involved, anyway. There are procedures to be followed. Procedures are very important in an operation like this.

Max Procedures? You make it sound frightfully complicated, for a radio chat show.

Hector It's a measure of her professionalism. You don't get her kind of success, without it. The programme's at the top of the ratings. She has an enormous fan mail.

Max Fan mail! Christ, we live in an *Alice in Wonderland* world. I mean what the hell is her popularity built on? The fact that as a little scrubber of sixteen, she dropped her knickers for some greasy half-wit who could just about string together a few chords on an electric guitar.

Hector That, if you don't mind me saying so, is a bit rich coming from someone with such a patrician view of the media. I doubt that even our nastiest tabloid would have described Amelia's success in those terms. I would remind you that she has a first class honours in English Literature, and that her novel, "The Beggar's Inheritance", was top of the best sellers list for nearly a year.

Max But not even a sniff at Booker or Whitbread. And we know why, don't we? Because, unlike the literati of the airport departure lounge, the organisers of those competitions know that it takes more than a good fuck on every third page, and a sprinkling of designer names, to make a satisfactory, let alone a great, novel.

Hector Really, that is a travesty! The fact is the literary establishment of this country despises popular success. Jeffrey Archer, for instance ——

Max Oh, please, spare me Jeffrey Archer.

Hector My point, precisely. (*Pause*) And your description of Jake Milo hardly squares with his standing as one of the world's most respected rock musicians; a man who has raised millions of pounds for charity; a man honoured with an OBE; a man whose eighteen years of marriage to Amelia have passed without the slightest hint of impropriety.

Max And the drugs? You seem, conveniently, to have overlooked that little episode in Jake Milo's distinguished career.

Hector Not at all. He has made no secret of it.

Max Secret? The man's made a bloody career out of it.

Hector He was a young man. And given his milieu, experimentation with drugs was hardly surprising. Certainly it was a bad time in his life — a tragic time ——

Max He survived ——

Hector Yes, but ——

Max — which is more than those kids did.

Hector You have no right to say that. There was never any evidence to suggest that Jake Milo had anything to do with that tragic incident. The Coroner made it quite clear in his summing-up ——

Max Yes, yes, we all know about that. But all the same ——

Hector Quite. But for someone who holds Amelia and Jake in such obvious contempt, you were, if I may say so, not backward in coming forward, when the invitation to come on the programme was issued.

Max My dear chap, I am a politician, and politics is a trade where one cannot afford to be too fastidious about the company one keeps. But as you have already acknowledged, I am a politician of some standing ——

Hector A Prime Minister-in-waiting, some say.

Max's reaction tells us that this is news to him, but that the idea is an attractive one which he cannot entirely reject

Max That's as maybe. But I had expected Ms Cruikshank to be here, if only to welcome me on her programme. Instead, I am left to kick my heels for fifteen minutes, in a room that has all the welcoming ambience of a police interview room.

Hector It strikes you like that?

Max Well, I mean — look at it. How would you describe it?

Hector I would describe it as utilitarian. A place suitable for preliminary interviews. Somewhere to deal with the files.

Max Preliminary? Interview? Files? You make it sound all very …

Hector Interrogational? I suppose it does, rather. (*Pause*) Does that bother you?

Max I have no intention of being interrogated by you or anyone else.

Hector No question of that, I assure you! (*Pause*) Tell you what, why don't we go straight into the first piece of music? Break the ice. We do seem to have got off to a rather tetchy start.

Max (*not sure whether to stay*) Well, I don't ——

Hector Oh, come on! You know it's in your own interest. I mean, a guest on the Amelia Cruikshank show. A radio show that competes in the ratings with the best TV soaps. It's a phenomenon. You can't afford not to be part of it. (*Pause*) Now, let me take your coat. Then we'll get started.

Hector takes Max's coat; Max seems reluctant to part with it

Mozart, wasn't it? Piano Sonata in C major, K545.

Max How the hell did you know that?

Hector hangs up the coat and goes to the desk, ushering Max into the chair on the other side. They sit

Hector As I said, Amelia's very careful on background research.

Max But I don't ——

Hector Christmas 1938, wasn't it? You'd have been about four. Your favourite aunt takes you to see the Christmas lights in the West End. Just before the lights went out all over Europe. Finished the evening in Lyons Corner House, Oxford Street. Downstairs in the Brasserie, where the orchestra played while you had your meal. Must have been very exciting for you. They played that tune. Of course they gave it a different name. (*He searches through his file*) Let's see, what was it … ?

Max "Eighteenth Century Drawing-Room." But I don't understand. How … ?

Hector "Eighteenth Century Drawing Room"! Of course. That's it. Charming. Really charming. (*He scribbles a note in the file*) Actually, Amelia thought it would be rather a good wheeze if we started with the arrangement, then mixed in the actual sonata. (*He closes the file*) What do you think?

Max (*perplexed*) Think? Well, I suppose … But look, I still don't ——

Hector Damned annoying though ——

Max (*completely lost*) Annoying? I really don't understand.

Hector Our library — not being able to run a recording of the arrangement to ground. I can tell you Amelia is pretty miffed with them. (*Pause*) Yes, damned annoying. (*Pause*) But we'll get it in time for the interview, never fear. (*Pause*) Yes, I think Amelia's idea will really work.

Max But I still don't see. I mean, how on earth —— ?

Hector Thought we'd have the actual sonata anyway — a few bars, just to get the feeling of things.

Hector presses the play button on the tape machine, which plays the opening of the Mozart C major piano sonata, K545. While the music is playing, Max sits numbly, staring straight ahead. Hector opens his file and turns the pages. Something catches his eye. With sudden decision, he leans forward and presses the stop button on the machine

Hector A happy childhood? Would you say you had a happy childhood?

Max (*snapping back to consciousness*) What?

Hector Was it a happy childhood? I mean that's important, don't you think?

Max Important?

Hector A secure childhood — important in the way we develop into adults. Don't you agree? After all, you were a father, yourself.

Max Father? Yes ——

Hector So yours was a happy one?

Max is very tense. He seems to struggle with the question. Then, with sudden relaxation, he is his old, confident self

Max *Children's Hour*!

Hector *Children's Hour*?

Max On the wireless. *Children's Hour*. One of the things I remember about that period. Uncle Mac, Toy Town, that sort of thing.

Hector Bit before my time. I'm one of the *Blue Peter* generation.

Max The wireless fed the imagination. Had to create your own pictures.

Hector (*flicking through the file*) Yes, of course. There was this schoolboy detective. Strange name. Now what was it? (*He finds the name in the file*) Yes, that's it. Bunkle.

Max (*leaping to his feet in a fury*) What the hell's going on here? (*He leans across the desk and tries to grab the file*) Give me those papers!

Hector (*pulling the file to his chest and wrapping his arms around it protectively*) Please, please! Do try to control yourself.

Max (*with another attempt to grab the file*) Give me that bloody file! You have no right.

Hector Oh, but we do. We have every right. (*Pause*) Now please return to your seat. This sort of outburst really will not do.

Max sits down slowly

Max I want to see that file.

Hector I'm afraid that's out of the question. It's departmental policy. The subject is never allowed access to his or her file.

Max (*getting to his feet again and pacing about the room*) Jesus Christ! What is this? Departmental policy? The subject? I thought this was a commercial radio station. You make it sound like something out of Kafka.

Hector Oh, come now. It strikes me that your imagination was, perhaps, a little overfed by all those exciting radio plays.

Max It's nothing to do with that. It's all this talk of ——

Hector (*holding up his hands in mock surrender*) All right, perhaps my choice of terminology was, in the circumstances, somewhat inflated. Amelia has often commented on my propensity to use the language of the bureaucrat. (*Pause*) I don't think she approves. (*Pause*) You see, there was a time, when I left university ... Well, I had rather hoped ... The Treasury, perhaps — or the FCO — or, maybe ——

Max The Ministry of State Security?

Hector But there isn't ... Oh. I see. Just your little joke.

Max Yes, just my little joke.

Hector Well, shall we get on? I say, won't you sit down? You standing about like that — makes me a bit uncomfortable.

Max remains standing

(*With a shrug*) Very well. Please yourself. (*He glances at the open file*) This young Bunkle chap was, it seems, responsible for introducing you to one of the greatest musical loves of your life, Elgar.

Max The signature tune of the series: *Chanson de Matin.* (*Softly, almost to himself*) It seemed so — secure. A happy world, full of sunshine, that would go on and on.

Hector presses the play button on the tape machine. Elgar's "Chanson de Matin" plays. Just for a moment, Max seems transported by the pleasure of it. Hector, on the other hand, appears slightly bored. He continues to flick through the file. But Max's countenance changes to a wild, almost demented look. He rushes over to the desk, grabs Hector by the throat, and hauls him to his feet

Hector (*struggling*) What on earth … ?

Max I know what this is. You're some fiendish scientist! You've put things in my head.

Hector (*trying to break Max's grip*) For God's sake, man!

Max Things in my head! That's what you've done!

Hector Have you gone mad?

Max I was perfectly sane when I came in here. But now you've put things in my head.

Hector (*struggling*) But that's ——

Max Probes in my head; that's what you've done. How else could you know what I'm thinking? You can see — see into my head.

In desperation, Hector manages to throw a punch. It catches Max on the face. Max lets go of Hector and reels away across the room. He stands, his back to the audience, leaning forwards, holding his face in his hands. Hector stands, massaging his neck and trying to get his breath. When he's regained some control of himself, he presses the stop button on the tape machine

Hector (*still having difficulty getting his breath*) Are you all right?

Max slowly straightens up and turns. There is blood around his nose

Max What have you done to my head?

Hector My dear chap, I've bloodied your nose. I'm most awfully sorry, but I really thought you were trying to kill me.

Max You've put things in my head.

Hector I punched you on the nose. I assure you, apart from that, I've done nothing to your head.

Max Then how do you know these things?

Hector It's really quite simple. Nothing in your head. Just a note on the file, nothing more sinister than that. (*He takes a handkerchief from the breast pocket of his jacket and dampens it with water from the jug*) Here, let me try to clean you up.

Max Note on the file? But I still don't understand.

Hector Oh, come on. Sit down. Let me see to that mess on your face. I'll explain.

Max comes to the table and sits. Hector dabs at Max's face with the wet handkerchief during the following

Good, I think the bleeding has stopped. But the nose is looking rather sore. What will people say? You come on the Amelia ——
Max The note on the file?
Hector There, soon have it sorted out. Perhaps I'll ring down to First Aid. Just to be on the safe ——
Max (*pushing Hector away, violently*) Leave my fucking nose alone! (*He pulls out his own handkerchief and dries his face during the following*) This file note. Where did it come from? And what is the source of the information it contains?
Hector (*returning to his chair and glancing down at the file*) Look. I really don't know what all the fuss is about. It's simply based on an interview you gave. All that stuff about musical milestones in your life.
Max Musical milestones? I've never given such an interview.
Hector But you did! You must remember. It was only ——
Max (*firmly*) I have never given such an interview. (*Pause. Then, getting to his feet*) I want to see Ms Cruikshank. I am not at all satisfied with the way ——

The telephone rings. Hector answers it. During the following speech, Max moves to collect his coat

Hector (*into the telephone, with obvious annoyance*) Yes? (*He listens for a moment*) Well, these things can't be rushed. (*He listens again, with increasing annoyance. He gets to his feet, turns away from Max and frowns up at the wall behind his chair*) Really, do you take me for a complete idiot? ... Oh, very well. If you think it'll help. (*He replaces the receiver; to Max*) Well, perhaps it's for the best, bringing things to a halt for the time being. I gather there's someone else waiting to come into this room. Interview with another distinguished politician, as a matter of fact. Sebastian Elwood.
Max Elwood? On this programme? You can't be serious.
Hector Not quite your ideological cup of tea, I guess.

Max That little shit is a disgrace to politics.

Hector Yes, well, Amelia thinks it's right to keep a political balance in her programme. It's a pity we weren't able to finish, but ——

Max (*putting his coat back on the coatstand and returning to sit in his chair*) But we are going to finish. I've given up a good deal of valuable time this morning. I'm not having it wasted, just because some moron is waiting about outside.

Hector (*doubtfully*) Well, I'm not sure. Perhaps another day.

Max No, I insist. If I have to leave now, you can forget the whole thing.

Hector I'll see what can be done. (*He picks up the telephone and dials. There is a brief pause. Into the phone*) Hallo. … Yes. Look it's Hector. I was wondering whether we could hang on in here for a while longer. Just to complete things. … Yes, yes, I quite understand that. But well, quite frankly, if we have to finish now, Sir Max has made it clear he's not prepared to go on with the programme. … (*Indignantly*) Well it wasn't my fault the beastly file went missing. … Really? I say, thanks. … Yes, yes. Soon as poss. (*He puts the telephone down*) So, that's all right. They're going to shunt Elwood into a standby room. (*With a laugh*) Believe me, by comparison, this place is five star luxury!

Max Good. Put the little shit in his place.

Hector Shall we get on then? I did say we wouldn't be too long.

Max Fire away.

Hector The woman who became your wife.

Max Rachel.

Hector You first met her, I believe … (*He glances at the file*)

Max In 1954. At a party in the rooms of one of my university friends.

Hector And the music you associate with falling in love? Something played at the party?

Max No. The music that will always conjure up that happiest of summers for me is Gene Kelly singing *Our Love Is Here to Stay*, from the film *An American in Paris*.

Hector You saw the film with Rachel?

Max Our first date. Some weeks after our first meeting. We saw it at the Hampstead Everyman. That scene, where Gene Kelly walks Leslie Caron under the bridges, beside the Seine — and that song — so romantic ...

Hector starts the tape machine and Gene Kelly is heard singing "Our Love Is Here To Stay" (Words: Ira Gershwin. Music: George Gershwin)

(*Nodding appreciatively*) Couldn't get it out of my head. And after the film. We strolled up Heath Street to the restaurant where we had supper, I had no doubt: this was the woman I wanted to spend the rest of my life with. *Our Love Is Here To Stay*; that was playing in my mind, when I asked her to marry me. (*He sits back in his chair, eyes closed, listening to the music, drifting back into his memories*)

Hector lets Max listen for a few moments, then stops the tape

Hector You were married, I believe, within a few weeks.
Max Before I went back to Cambridge.
Hector But you didn't complete your degree?
Max Had to get a job. Rachel was pregnant by the time I'd got to the third term of my second year.
Hector The first great tragedy in your life.
Max No! No! Not the pregnancy. It wasn't planned, true. But the thought of a child was a happiness, a real happiness.
Hector But the happiness that became your daughter, Judith, was also the tragedy that was the loss of Rachel.

Max leans forward, elbows on the table, head in hands

Max (*very softly*) The music.
Hector (*puzzled*) The music?
Max (*without looking up*) I want the music.

In confusion, Hector turns the pages of the file

Hector But there is no music scheduled here.
Max *Traviata.*

Hector *Traviata?* (*He has another rapid look through the file*) I don't understand. There's no mention of *Traviata*. There must be some mistake, the file says nothing about *Traviata*.

Max (*looking up; triumphantly*) So there is nothing in my head. Can't be, or you'd have known I was going to ask for *Traviata*.

Hector For God's sake, man! I've already told you, we've put nothing in your head. It's all here in the file.

Max Well, you've got to admit, my scheme worked. Flushed out you and your nasty little file.

Hector (*irritably*) Yes, yes. Frightfully clever. (*Pause*) Look, we really don't have much time. Perhaps we could get on.

Max *Traviata.*

Hector (*in exasperation*) We had no warning — nothing on file.

Max Act III duet. You know, where Alfredo has just returned to find Violetta dying.

Hector I'm not very well up on opera.

Max But his arrival seems to revive her and they sing of the time when she will be well again, and they can go back to their home in the country.

Hector (*gesturing at the tape player*) But I don't have it. How was I to know?

Max Well, get it. I mean it shouldn't be that difficult for a major radio station.

Hector Of course not. It's just ... Well, as I've already explained, we don't have much time.

Max Why don't you get your library Johnnies on to it? We can continue the discussion while we're waiting.

Hector I'll see what I can do. (*He picks up the telephone and dials. Into the phone*) Oh, hallo. Hector here again. ... Look, I wonder, do you think that someone could pop along to the library to get a particular piece of music? ... Yes, I know. But Sir Max is most anxious that we should include it. ... Duet from the third act of *La Traviata*. ... You will? That's excellent. Thanks. ... No, really. We won't be too long now. (*He puts the telephone down*) They'll see what they can do.

Max Thank you.

Hector *Traviata?* Something to do with Rachel's death?

Max They knew there were going to be difficulties from quite early on in the pregnancy. Tried to persuade her to terminate. But she wouldn't hear of it. She was rushed to hospital a month before the baby was due. It was the most frightful period of my life. Then, quite suddenly, the child was born. A beautiful daughter — as healthy as you could wish for. I went to see Rachel. Chap took me to one side before I got to her; said I had to prepare myself ... The whole business, a terrible strain ... Nothing they could do. (*Pause*) But I wasn't taking any of that crap. The child, my Judith, was fine — so why not the mother? (*He drifts away into his own thoughts*)

There is a pause

Hector (*in an attempt to get things started again*) So you had to bring up the baby on your own?

Max (*not conscious of Hector's question, carrying on where he left off*) I really think that seeing me gave her, if only for a moment, the will to live. The spark was there to see. I took her in my arms. Tried to fan the spark into a flame. It glowed brightly — then died. (*Pause*) So you see, that's why I want *Traviata*.

Hector If you ask me, it's typical Italian sentimentality.

Max What do you mean?

Hector All that having the hero return just in time for a poignant farewell with the dying heroine. It's not how Dumas the younger saw it, in *La Dame aux Camélias*.

Max How do you know about the Dumas connection? I thought you weren't very well up on opera.

Hector You don't have to be very well up on the subject to know that. Have you read the novel?

Max shakes his head

I can tell you, the French take a harder-nosed view of things. In the novel, by the time he arrives she's already dead and buried. But he must see her again, so he has the body disinterred. (*Pause*) Imagine, gazing at the woman you adore, when the worms have

been at her for a few weeks. (*Pause*) They say it's the eyes, the fleshy part of the nose, and the lips that go first.
Max I think I'll stick to Verdi and sentimentality.
Hector (*with barely suppressed anger*) And I say, beware sentimentality. It's a characteristic of some of the most vicious tyrants in history.
Max But you'll get the music?
Hector I've said we will.
Max Good. That's kind of you.
Hector Now we must get on. I can't keep this room forever.
Max You want to know about bringing up Judith?
Hector You were very young. Only twenty-one. Wasn't there the temptation … ?
Max Temptation?
Hector To find someone to take over the child — maybe even adopt her? Rebuild your own life — finish your degree — marry again, perhaps.
Max The thought never entered my head. (*He leans across the table, now interrogational*) Have you ever loved? I mean really loved?

Hector remains silent, but looks uncomfortable

I thought not. You don't look the sort of man who might love. Too enamoured of your tidy little files and neat procedures. But love? Ah, my friend, there's danger there. A man might spill his guts because of love. (*Pause. He takes a long, hard look at Hector*) That's if he has guts to spill.

Hector, embarrassed, shuffles the papers in the file

Hector So what about bringing up the baby?
Max I had to get someone in. Mrs Price. Six days a week. But at nights and on Sundays, we, Judith and I, were a single-parent family — long before they became the flavour of the *fin de siècle.*
Hector But was there no … No … Well, resentment?

Max Resentment? (*Pause*) My God, what a conventional little man you are. You berate me for my sentimentality; well, perhaps I do stand guilty of that. But at least sentimentality implies an awareness of life, a reaction to it, however misguided. Far better that than the mean, petty-mindedness of the grubby little clerk. Only such a man could conceive of resentment against a child, the flesh of a woman so passionately loved; a child who daily grew, gloriously, to recreate that woman.

Hector Recreate her? You saw the child in those terms?

Max (*leaping to his feet*) What the hell do you mean by that?

Hector I was merely interested in what you said.

Max (*starting towards the door*) I've had enough of you and your insinuating questions.

Hector (*standing*) Oh, come now! What insinuation? I was only ——

Max (*in angry mimicry*) "Recreate her? You saw the child in those terms?" (*Pause*) I know what you're thinking, you bastard! Well, you're wrong. It was never like that.

Hector I assure you — look, this really is very silly.

Max moves to collect his coat. Hector watches him in an obvious state of panic, trying to think how to stop Max leaving. In what is a sudden desperate throw, he presses the play button on the tape machine. The music is the Flanders and Swann "Song of the Gnu" —from the point at which the song is introduced with the words, "A little animal song". Immediately, Max stops what he is doing. He stands for a moment, motionless, listening. Then, on tip-toe, he begins to move about the room, as though searching for a hidden child. Whenever the song reaches the words, "I'm a Gnu", Max sings them too. As he does, he pounces as though having found the hiding place. He then chases the imaginary child, making exaggerated grabbing motions, and singing "I'm a Gnu", every time the song comes to those words. (NB There should be nothing sinister or in any way threatening about this pantomime. It should represent nothing more than a father playing a game with his happy young child) As the first verse comes to an end, Max runs out of steam; he sinks to his knees and, head in hands, sobs, uncontrollably.

Hector stands watching. He lets the music play on for a while, then stops it

Hector (*quietly*) I'm sorry.

Max doesn't seem to have heard. Slowly, he takes control of himself

I said, I'm sorry.
Max (*looking up, wiping a hand over his eyes*) Sorry?
Hector What I said. About Judith. I implied that there might have been something not quite right in your relationship with her. I had no right.

Max gets to his feet. He seems undecided what to do, but comes to sit back at the desk. It's as if he hasn't the strength to do anything else

Max Forget it.

Hector resumes his seat

Hector But it must have been difficult, all the same. Bringing up a young girl when you were busy building a career. And adolescence — difficult enough for parents at the best of times, but in Judith's case, she'd have reached it at the end of the sixties. Explosion of youth culture. Rejection of social mores. The pressure on her, and you, must have been enormous.
Max (*briskly; not wanting to pursue the subject*) We coped. Anyway, she was never much into all that pop music.
Hector (*glancing at the file*) So it seems. Ballet was her love.
Max Since she was very young. She could have only been five, when I first took her to Covent Garden. *La Fille mal Gardée.*
Hector Which brings us to the next piece of music. The Clog Dance from *La Fille mal Gardée*. I can just imagine how a young child would have loved it.

Hector starts the tape machine. The Clog Dance from "La Fille mal Gardée" (Hérold) plays

Max (*talking over the music*) She did. It was, I suppose — that dreadful cliché — a defining moment in her life. Couldn't wait to start ballet classes.

Hector (*talking over the music*) I believe she took it very seriously. Kept up the classes, until ——

Max She had real talent. Her teachers said so. Could have gone all the way to the top.

Hector stops the tape

Hector In a strange way, that first ballet was rather apt, don't you think?

Max How do you mean, apt?

Hector *La Fille mal Gardée* — "The badly guarded daughter". In the circumstances, some might consider that apt. Tragically apt, perhaps — but apt nonetheless.

Max (*heatedly*) What was I supposed to do? You try to protect — to bring them up with an understanding of right and wrong. But in the end, you have to let go. She was seventeen, for God's sake, a mature, level-headed young woman — until she met that worm.

Hector Some project initiated by the dance school, I believe? A fusion of ballet and rock music.

Max Look, I really don't want to talk about that. Can't we just — ?

Hector And is it true you sued the school? Breach of their responsibility to maintain the moral well-being of the young people in their charge. (*With a laugh*) Moral well-being? That was a bit of a flyer, wasn't it? I mean, that sort of litigation might be all right in the States, but ——

Max A flyer? (*He jumps up in a fury*) You bloody little runt! A flyer? You may find the concept of moral well-being amusing, but it wasn't your daughter who became enmeshed in the web of filth that was Jake Milo. Yes, I sued. I wanted to take them for every penny they had. It was their duty to protect my child from monsters like him.

Hector Monster? Oh, come now, that's nonsense. Jake Milo was no monster.

Max You think not? Then tell me how you would describe a man who takes a seventeen year old girl, a beautiful, intelligent girl, full of life, and with all of life ahead of her — a man who takes this girl and turns her into a drunken, drug-crazed whore?

Hector There was never any evidence to link Jake to your daughter's behaviour.

Max Oh, there was evidence all right! The evidence of my eyes. That night when I came home and found the pair of them in my bed, the bed I had once shared with her mother, she was so far gone on drugs and booze, that she didn't even recognize the man who threw her into the street.

Hector Hardly the behaviour of a concerned parent wanting to help his daughter through a difficult period in her life.

Max Concerned parent? All I could think of was the need to burn that bed.

Hector You're surely not telling me that it was the first indication you had that something was wrong?

Max Of course I'd noticed some changes; changes which I might not have particularly liked. But you've got to give them room — room to make the odd mistakes, even. I had confidence in her basic maturity.

Hector So you just stood by and watched — watched the slide into drunken, drug-crazed whoring? (*Pause. Holding up his hands in a mock-defensive manner*) I only use the terminology you yourself employed.

Max Stood by? Christ, you make it sound as though I had nothing else to do.

Hector Ah, I wondered when we'd get around to the things that might have distracted you from your daughter's plight.

Max All right, all right! It was an important time in my career.

Hector Your first junior Ministerial post.

Max Yes, well, I can tell you, when those opportunities come up, you grab them. There are no second chances.

Hector So, whilst the nation's farming community profited from what was, I am sure, your vast experience in matters agricultural, your daughter lost what she might reasonably have expected: the concern and support of a loving parent.

Max I reject that — categorically! I did all I reasonably could.

Hector No, you didn't. In fact the first real action you took, and that was negative, was when you discovered that they'd soiled your precious nuptial bed.

Max (*becoming agitated and pacing about the room*) And ransacked the drinks cupboard ... Carpets covered in cigarette ash and half-eaten food ... Bath overflowing ... Grafitti — and, and —— (*He runs out of steam and stops across the room from where Hector sits. His breath comes in short gasps. He is clearly in a very emotional state*)

Hector Time for some music, I think. (*He starts the tape machine*)

Music plays; the opening of the slow movement of the Elgar Cello Concerto

Hector So what does this bring to mind?

Max Bring to mind? I don't know what you mean.

Hector Oh, but you do. It wasn't very long ago. Only the day before yesterday, in fact.

Max Day before yesterday?

Hector Or perhaps yesterday. Yes, perhaps it seems like only yesterday. Come on, try to remember.

Max stands in torment. We see that he knows there is something to remember, but he doesn't want it. He must keep it in his subconscious, where he has buried it

You were playing it, when you left her in the flat, that evening.

Max (*desperately*) No!

Hector Oh, but yes. (*Coaxingly*) Now, what was it she said?

Max Said?

Hector You remember. About the music. What did she say about the music?

Max appears to be in a trance, struggling with the returning memory during the following

(*Very quietly*) Listen to the music, Max. Listen carefully. You
remember. What did she say about it?
Max She said …
Hector Yes?
Max She said … She said … She said it was one of her favourites.
Hector Yes! That's good. That's very good! And what did you say?
Max I said I doubted that anyone of her limited imagination would
be able to appreciate music of that emotional intensity.
Hector (*glancing at the file*) That's right. You did say that. Exactly
that. Good. Very good. Now we're getting somewhere. *(He stops
the tape, goes to Max and takes him by the arm)* Come on now,
old chap, why don't you sit down?

*Max, still in a trance-like state, allows himself to be led back to his
chair, where he sits down. Hector goes back to his side of the desk
and sits down*

So what happened, then? (*In a gentle, coaxing voice*) Come on,
now. You were doing so well. What happened then?
Max I can't remember. Why don't you ask her?
Hector We'd like to. But you see … Well, to tell the truth, we rather
seem to have lost contact with her.
Max Lost contact?
Hector Precisely. Lost contact. Since Thursday evening. That was
when she came to see you, wasn't it?

Max remains silent

Naturally, we were concerned — next morning when she didn't
turn up at the office. We checked. Not at her flat. Porter confirmed
she hadn't been home all night. He said that was unusual. Even
suggested that with Jake being away in the States, on tour … Well,
you know: nudge, nudge, wink, wink. (*Pause*) I think that's rather
impertinent, don't you?

Still Max doesn't respond

Bloody impertinent, in fact. I mean that's a position of trust. We could have been anyone — reporters on some tabloid. (*Pause*) Well, as you might imagine, we were left in a bit of a tiz. You were our next port of call. Couldn't raise you on the telephone, but we went round to the flat, just in case. No-one at home. Neighbour says she recognized Amelia, getting out of a taxi, outside the main entrance to the flats, at eight-thirty the previous evening. That fitted in all right — eight-thirty was the time of her appointment with you. So what happened after that? Something of a mystery. (*Pause*) Bit naughty, I suppose, but do you know what we did?

There is no response from Max. He might not even be listening

We broke in. Of course we were very careful. Not like some — you know, really turn a place over. I call that unprofessional. Except when it's done deliberately, to put the frighteners on someone — flush them out. Yes, sometimes that's done. But in your case, we just wanted a quiet look around. (*Pause*) It all seemed very normal. Just a nice, tidy flat. In fact the only thing we found out of place was something that seemed to have slipped down behind one of the chairs. Would you like to see what it was?

Max still shows no sign of interest

(*Opening the desk drawer, bringing out a Filofax-type notebook in a sealed plastic bag and holding it up*) See, this is what we found.

Max glances at the bag, but immediately looks away

Funny, when you think about it. I mean, someone as high-powered as Amelia Cruikshank; you'd think she would use a tape machine for interviews. But she's dead set against them. Thinks they make the subject — whoops, there I go again — the interviewee — she thinks they make the interviewee uncomfortable. She writes it all down, in almost minute detail. So you see, we didn't have to put things in your head — we had

Amelia's notes of the interview. But the intriguing thing is, they stop at *La Fille mal Gardée*. Surely that wasn't the end? Not with so much of your life and times left untouched. (*He waits for Max to respond*)

There is nothing

I wonder, could it be something to do with the fact that with *La Fille mal Gardée* the story had reached the point where your life and Amelia's touched, albeit indirectly? Had the conversation begun to turn on matters that Amelia thought best left unrecorded?

Still no response from Max

And now she's disappeared. (*He gets up and goes to stand behind Max's chair. He leans over Max's shoulder and speaks in quiet, confidential tones*) Of course, you may have had nothing to do with her disappearance. But finding the notebook in your flat … Well, that does raise certain questions. I mean, Amelia isn't the sort to leave her notes on an important interview behind. No, that's not like her at all. Then there's the abrupt end to the interview. I can tell you, that really set me thinking. What might you have been talking about?

Max appears to be about to say something

Yes?

But Max returns to motionlessly staring ahead

Then it came to me. How could I have been so blind? There was only one subject which fitted the bill. Murder. The murder of your daughter, Judith, and the two other girls, all those years ago. Of course, it was never officially categorized as murder, but the Coroner left his verdict open. There was a strong suspicion that it wasn't just an accident that the three girls got hold of the adulterated drugs. But who? Who would have done a terrible thing like that? You had your suspicions, didn't you?

Max (*with a struggle*) It was ...

Hector waits, but Max lapses back into silence. Hector shrugs and perches on the edge of the table

Hector Jake Milo? Bit far-fetched, wasn't it? What motive? Particularly since the only one of the trio he knew was your daughter. And he hadn't seen Judith for at least a week — shacked up in a cottage in Wales, with his latest love, the sixteen year old Amelia Cruikshank. And her evidence was that he was stoned out of his mind for most of that time. (*Pause*) Oh, that's not to say there weren't plenty of good solid citizens who were rooting for you. The death of three upper-middle-class girls would have been a small price to pay, to see one of those stinking punk rockers sent down for life. But it wasn't Jake, was it? I think you knew who it really was — and I think Amelia did as well.

Max (*struggling for words*) It wasn't like ... (*He gives up the struggle and falls silent again*)

Hector Not like that. Is that what you're trying to say? I think it was. (*He returns to stand behind Max's chair. He leans forward, as though to whisper in Max's ear*) She wouldn't let go, would she? And when Amelia gets on to something, she pursues it with a forensic intensity.

Max (*becoming increasingly agitated, fighting to get the words out*) She ... She said ...

Hector (*with increasing excitement in his voice*) It must have been a terrible blow. The girl, your beautiful daughter, in whom you had invested so much hope. Star of the Royal Ballet, brilliant hostess at dinner parties for the cream of British — no, not just British, *international* society. The girl who was so much like the only woman you had ever loved. All of that suddenly gone. Replaced by a filthy slut. Eyes glazed, hardly able to stand, and who, if she recognized her father at all, could only mouth obscenities at him. Could your love for her stand that pornography? Or was it the trigger that released the resentment you had locked away so carefully — the resentment towards the creature that had been responsible for the death of your beloved Rachel?

Max leaps to his feet and lunges at Hector in an explosive movement

Max Bloody damn you! No! No! No!

Hector overcomes Max's attack with the ease of a professional. He pins Max's arms behind him, and forces him over the back of the chair

Hector (*shouting in his excitement*) Amelia knew it all, didn't she? How you got hold of the stuff. These things can be arranged discreetly for a man with your contacts. How it was passed to the girls. Every little detail. Yes, she knew it all.

There is a knock at the door

(*Too carried away to hear*) And how sweet, if you could have pinned it on Jake.

There is another knock, this time more urgent. Still Hector doesn't hear

Oh, she's a smart one, is Amelia. Of course, she wasn't going to expose you. That's not her style. But if there's one thing Amelia likes, it's the power to influence things. So there would have been a price to pay.

There is more knocking, more insistent than before

And you couldn't have that, could you? So you killed her. Isn't that what —— ?

The door opens and a Messenger comes into the room

What the —— ?

Hector looks up to see the Messenger. Abruptly, he lets go of Max and walks away, like a bully caught in the act, trying to distance himself from the violence

Hasn't anyone told you to knock before you enter an interview room?

Messenger I did knock. I knocked three times.

Hector Then you should have waited, until I called you in.

Messenger But they said it was important. Get it to you straight away. (*He holds up a tape cassette*) That's what they told me. (*Pause*) Three times, I knocked.

Hector Put it on the table and get the hell out of here.

The Messenger puts the tape on the desk and leaves

There is a long silence. Max stands facing the audience, totally impassive. Hector, on the other hand, seems to have been completely thrown off course by the interruption. He wanders about the room in an aimless way; stops to flick through the file. He seems to be on the point of saying something, but checks himself. He moves to his side of the desk, remaining standing

Max (*very quietly*) It wasn't like that.

Hector (*struggling to regain concentration*) What's that?

Max I didn't kill my daughter.

Hector (*with a sneer*) Oh, yes, we know. It was Jake Milo.

Max Not Jake Milo.

This is enough to bring Hector back to full alertness

Hector Not Jake? Then who —— ?

Max It was her.

Hector Her?

Max Amelia.

Hector (*incredulously*) Amelia!? Oh, for Christ's sake!

Max (*in an absolutely flat voice*) Amelia Cruikshank murdered Judith.

Hector (*his certainty undermined*) But that's nonsense! Why on earth —— ?

Max Had to get Judith out of the way. She wanted Jake to herself.

Hector Oh, come on! Jake had already given Judith up when he met Amelia.

Max Not so. That's the story Amelia put about and, in the circumstances, Jake had no choice but to confirm it.

Hector Circumstances?

Max He was trapped by her. That famous alibi she provided. She persuaded him that it was a lie, that he really did murder those girls. And for all he knew, it was true … That week with Amelia in Wales … A blackout, so far as he was concerned. She'd seen to that.

Hector This all sounds rather far-fetched.

Max Eighteen years of marriage without the slightest hint of impropriety. Isn't that how you described it? Now you know why. Not that she was in any way inhibited; needs must when the devil drives. I gather there's something of a gap between Jake's macho image and his performance.

Hector She couldn't have kept up the pretence. Not for all that time. Something would have given.

Max That woman murdered Judith, and came to mock my impotence. So I —— (*He shoots out his arms to their full reach, and his hands grab an imaginary throat*)

Hector is shocked by the suddenness and violence of this action

Hector You strangled her? With your bare hands?

During the following, Max mimes increasing the pressure on the imaginary throat

Max All the time I watched her face. Her face — that mean little face. First it was just fear, that I might hurt her. Then as the breathing became more difficult, and she realized that I meant business, panic. The more she struggled, the worse it became. Eyes pleading, until they began to bulge; tongue lolling from between those thin, penny-pinching lips. Then her hands slipped off my wrists and her body was limp. (*Pause. In a slightly puzzled voice*) So soon? Was that all? (*He pushes the imaginary body* *away with a contemptuous gesture*) For the third time in my life, I had been robbed by death. (*He is suddenly drained. He looks blankly ahead*)

Hector (*opening the file and picking up a pen*) What did you do with Amelia?

Max doesn't respond

The body; what did you do with it?

This time Max looks towards Hector, but he doesn't seem to comprehend what Hector is saying

Amelia's body. What did you do with it?

Max The body? I left it — (*he has to think about it*) — in Cambridgeshire, I think.

Hector In Cambridgeshire? You think?

Max No, I'm sure it was Cambridgeshire.

Hector Cambridgeshire, for Christ's sake! Can't you be just a bit more specific?

Max I had a speaking engagement in Lincoln. Left in the early hours. Amelia in the boot. Somewhere north of Cambridge ... Found a well-filled dike. Used the spare wheel as a weight. (*Pause*) Couldn't have been more than fifteen to twenty miles beyond Cambridge.

Hector (*scribbling in the file; with resignation*) In a well-filled dike, fifteen to twenty miles north of Cambridge. Well, that should be a doddle. (*He continues to take notes during the following*)

Max sits down on his chair. He sits quietly, staring straight at the audience, hands folded in his lap

Hector Lincoln, you say? So that's what you were doing in the Spalding area. The woman who phoned said your car had been parked in the lay-by, opposite her cottage, when she got up at seven. When it was still there, with you sitting in it, motionless, at midday, she got the police. Thought you'd topped yourself. (*Pause*) But it was nothing like that, was it? Just shut up shop, hadn't you?

Max They took me home.

Hector Back to your flat. They say you didn't speak at all during the journey.

Max Pleasant just to watch the country go by.

Hector You must have been exhausted.

Max Dirty, mainly. Needed to clean up.

Hector A good hot bath. Nothing like it.

Max Then sleep. Yes, then I needed sleep.

Hector They stayed. Kept an eye on you.

Max And this morning: breakfast with the *FT*. Never start the day without the *FT*.

Hector All of that. You had all of that.

Max It was kind of you. And the car to collect me; that was thoughtful. Not really feeling myself.

Hector finishes his file note. He sits back in his chair and watches Max for a few moments, then he picks up the telephone. But he does not dial. It is clear he has a direct connection. As he speaks he turns to look at the wall behind him

Hector (*into the phone*) OK? Get it all? … Good. Well, I think Sir Max is ready for the formal recording. Perhaps you'd send someone along to escort him. … Fine, but not too long. I could murder a pint.

Hector gives a final glance at the file then closes it. He notices the cassette left by the Messenger. On impulse, he removes the existing tape from the machine and replaces it with the new one. He presses the play button and the duet, "Parigi, o cara, noi lesceremo", from Act III of "La Traviata" plays. Hector sits back in his chair, hands clasped behind his head, listening. Max remains motionless

The duet develops. The Lights and music fade

FURNITURE AND PROPERTY LIST

On stage: Desk. *On it*: practical lamp, telephone, tape machine, water jug and glasses. *In drawer*: Filofax-type notebook in a sealed plastic bag
Two chairs
Coatstand. *On it*: **Max**'s overcoat
Max's case on floor
Financial Times for **Max**

Off stage: Official-looking file, pen (**Hector**)
Tape cassette (**Messenger**)

Personal: **Max**: watch
Hector: handkerchief in breast pocket

LIGHTING PLOT

Practical fittings required: desk lamp
One interior

To open: Desk lamp on with covering glow

No cues

EFFECTS PLOT

Cue 1   As play begins   (Page 1)
Play Prelude to Act I of "La Traviata"
    over stage speakers

Cue 2   **Hector** enters   (Page 1)
Fade music

Cue 3   **Hector** presses play button on tape machine   (Page 6)
Play opening of Mozart's Piano Sonata in C major,
    K545 as if from tape machine

Cue 4   **Hector** presses stop button on tape machine   (Page 8)
Cut music from tape machine

Cue 5   **Hector** presses play button on tape machine   (Page 8)
Play Elgar's "Chanson de Matin" as if from tape machine

Cue 6   **Hector** presses stop button on tape machine   (Page 9)
Cut music from tape machine

Cue 7   **Max**: "I am not at all satisfied with the way —— "(Page 10)
Telephone rings

Cue 8   **Hector** presses play button on tape machine   (Page 12)
Play Gene Kelly singing "Our Love Is Here to Stay"
    as if from tape machine

Cue 9   **Hector** presses stop button on tape machine   (Page 12)
Cut music from tape machine

Cue 10 **Hector** presses play button on tape machine   (Page 16)
Play Flanders and Swann's "Song of the Gnu"
    as if from tape machine

Cue 11   **Hector** presses stop button on tape machine   (Page 17)
           Cut music from tape machine

Cue 12   **Hector** presses play button on tape machine   (Page 18)
           Play Clog Dance from "La Fille Mal Gardée"
             as if from tape machine

Cue 13   **Hector** presses stop button on tape machine   (Page 18)
           Cut music from tape machine

Cue 14   **Hector** presses play button on tape machine   (Page 20)
           Play opening of slow movement of Elgar's Cello
             Concerto as if from tape machine

Cue 15   **Hector** presses stop button on tape machine   (Page 21)
           Cut music from tape machine

*Cue*16   **Hector** presses play button on tape machine   (Page 29)
           Play "Parigi, o cara, noi lesceremo" from Act III
             of "La Traviata" as if from tape machine

www.ingramcontent.com/pod-product-compliance
Ingram Content Group UK Ltd.
Pitfield, Milton Keynes, MK11 3LW, UK
UKHW021821150726
7214IPUK00017B/255